Y0-EQU-207

BIBLE PRAYERS

FOR

CHILDREN

BIBLE PRAYERS FOR CHILDREN

Edited By
Rev. Lawrence Brett

Illustrations By
P. Ghijsens

THE REGINA PRESS
NEW YORK

PRINTED IN BELGIUM

Nihil Obstat: Raymond E. Tortora
Censor Librorum

Imprimatur: Walter P. Kellenberg, D.D.
Bishop of Rockville Centre

September 18, 1974

1526

Illustrations © Copyright 1980 by H. Proost & Cie
Turnhout - Belgium

PRINTED IN BELGIUM

1. BEFORE I PRAY

Jesus said:
"Let the little children come to me,
and do not stop them.
The kingdom of heaven
belongs to children."

(Matthew 18:16)

I pray:
Dear Lord,
you are always with me.
I come to you now
to talk with you.
Listen to what I say.
I love you, Lord.

2. THE SIGN OF THE CROSS

When I pray
I make the sign of the Cross.
I want to show God
that I love him.
I know he lives inside me.

I say:
In the name of the Father
and of the Son
and of the Holy Spirit.
(Matthew 28:19)

Amen.

3. OUR FATHER

Jesus taught us how to pray.
This is what Jesus taught us to say:

Our Father
who art in heaven,
hallowed be thy name.
Thy kingdom come.
Thy will be done on earth
as it is in heaven.
Give us this day our daily bread
and forgive us our trespasses,
as we forgive those who trespass against us.
And lead us not into temptation,
but deliver us from evil. Amen.

(Matthew 6:9-13)

CREDO

4. I BELIEVE

One day a man said to Jesus:
"I believe!
Help me to believe more!"

(Mark 9:24)

I say:
I believe in God the Father.
He made heaven and earth and all things.
I believe in God the Son.
He came to earth to save all men.
I believe in God the Holy Spirit.
He lives within my heart.
There is only one God —
The Father, Son and Holy Spirit.

5. HAIL MARY

Mary was the mother of Jesus.
Jesus loved her
just as we love our mothers.
We love Mary because we love Jesus.
She is
"the most blessed of all women."

(Luke 1:42)

I pray to her and say:

Hail Mary, full of grace.
The Lord is with thee.
Blessed art thou among women,
and blessed is the fruit of thy womb,
Jesus.
Holy Mary, mother of God,
pray for us sinners now
and at the hour of our death.
Amen.

6. MORNING PRAYER

I say this prayer to you, Lord,
for you listen for my voice
when day begins. *(Psalm 5:3)*

I pray to God as soon as I wake up.
I tell him:
Dear Lord, live in me this day.
Bless all that I shall do or say.
Shine within me like the sun,
Let me be good to everyone.

7. GUARDIAN ANGEL

Jesus said:
"The angels of heaven
are always with my heavenly Father."
(Matthew 18:10)

My Father in heaven loves me.
He protects me and wants me to be safe.
I pray:
Dear Father in heaven,
watch over me throughout each day.
One day let me join with all the angels
and sing your praises in heaven.

8. PRAYER AT MEALTIME

God sends rain from heaven.
He makes plants grow when they should.
He gives you food
and makes you happy. *(Acts 14:17)*

I thank God for giving us food,
and say:
Bless us, Lord, and these your gifts which we are about to receive from your goodness.
Through Christ our Lord. Amen.
May the Lord provide for the needs of others
and always be
our heavenly food. Amen.

9. DURING THE DAY

I should pray to God
throughout the day.
He told me:
"Everything you ask and pray for,
believe that you will have it,
and it will be yours." *(Mark 11:24)*

I pray:

Dear Lord, bless everyone
who sees me or hears me.
Bless everyone I love.
Bless all people
wherever they are.
Lead us all to heaven. Amen.

10. EVENING PRAYER

At night may a song be on my lips,
a prayer to God who gave me life.
(Psalm 42:8)

When day is over
I thank God for being with me:
I tell him:
Watch over me as I sleep,
dear Lord.
Watch over all who love you.
Give rest to all who are tired,
give food to all who are hungry,
and comfort all who are sick.
Amen.

11. THE CHURCH

Christ loved the Church
and gave his life for her
to make her holy. *(Ephesians 5:25)*

We should love the Church.
The Church is our mother.
The Church tells us
how to be holy.
I pray for the Church, and say:
Lord Jesus,
you love the Church very much.
Make her holy.
Help her bring
all people to heaven. Amen.

12. BAPTISM

There is one Lord, one faith,
and one baptism. *(Ephesians 4:5)*

When I was very small
my parents brought me to church.
Jesus made me his brother
when I was baptised.
I thank him, and say:
Dear Jesus, you are my brother.
Help me to know you better.
Teach all men to live
like your brothers. Amen.

13. CONFIRMATION

The love of God
has been poured into our hearts
by the Holy Spirit
who was given to us. *(Romans 5:5)*

The Sacrament of Confirmation
makes us strong Christians.
I pray:
Dear Lord, bless your people
who come to church to adore you.
Make them strong
and better Christians.
Help them
to love each other more.

14. HOLY MASS

The Mass is a meal.
Jesus feeds us
with his Body and Blood.
His Body looks like bread,
but it is really Jesus.
Jesus told us:
"Whoever eats this Bread
will live for ever." *(John 6:51)*

I thank him for this holy Food:
Dear Lord, you are my Food
when I receive you in Communion.
Help me to stay close to you
so that I can live for ever.
Amen.

15. CONFESSION

God wants me to be good.
Sometimes I am bad.
If I tell him I am sorry,
He will forgive me.
"You are good, Lord,
and ready to forgive." *(Psalm 86:5)*

I confess my sins to the priest,
and God forgives me all my sins.
I tell him I am sorry:
Dear God, I am sorry
that I have offended you.
I will try not to sin again.

16. CHRIST DIED FOR OUR SINS

Christ died for our sins,
just as the Scriptures
said he would. *(1 Corinthians 15:3)*

Jesus died on the Cross
to show us how much he loved us.
He died to forgive us
all our sins.
I thank him for what he did.
I say:
Dear Jesus, you died for me.
You love me very much.
I love you very much.
I will show you
how much I love you
by trying to be good.

17. I FORGIVE OTHERS

Jesus told us about a boy
who ran away from home,
but his father forgave him.
Jesus tells us:
"Forgive whatever you have
against anybody,
so your Father in heaven
will forgive you." *(Mark 11:25)*

I pray:
Dear Lord, I will do as you say.
I will forgive others
as you forgave me.
I will ask our Father in heaven
to forgive them as well. Amen.

18. CHRIST GAVE ME LIFE

Jesus rose from the dead
that we might live with his life.
The bible tells us:
"He has brought you
to life with him." *(Colossians 2:13)*

I thank Jesus for giving me life.
Dear Jesus,
you rose from the dead.
Now you live for ever.
May everyone live good lives.
May everyone live with you
for ever. Amen.

19. I HELP OTHERS

Jesus told us:
"Love one another
as I have loved you." *(John 14:34)*

If we do as Jesus told us,
we will try to love everybody.
We will try to be good and kind.
I pray:
Dear Lord, help me to love you.
Help all people
to love each other,
and to live as children of God.
Let us show this love
by helping those who need us.
Amen.

20. HEAVEN IS MY REAL HOME

Jesus promised us:
"You will eat and drink
at my table in the Kingdom."
(Luke 22:30)

If I am good,
Jesus will bring me to heaven,
and we will have a feast for ever.
I want to be with Jesus for ever.
I tell him:
Lord, be with me every day
throughout my life on earth.
Then may I be with you for ever
in the happiness of heaven.
For heaven is my real home. Amen.

PRINTED BY
proost Turnhout (Belgium)